illustrated guide to
COMMON ROCKS
and their minerals

REVISED EDITION

EDITOR
Brooking Tatum

ILLUSTRATIONS
Don Greame Kelley
Robert Edison

COLOR PHOTOGRAPHS
W. Scott Lewis

V. Brown
D. Allan

NATUREGRAPH

Library of Congress Cataloging in Publication Data

Allan, David, 1935–
  Illustrated guide to common rocks and their minerals.

Published in 1956 under title: An illustrated guide to common rocks and rock forming minerals.

Includes index.
1. Rocks—Handbooks, manuals, etc. 2. Mineralogy—Handbooks, manuals, etc. I. Brown, Vinson, 1912– joint author. II. Title.

QE432.A44 1976   549   76-7372

All the illustrations by Mr. Kelley, marked DonGK in the book, were originally published by Little, Brown & Co. in "The Amateur Naturalist's Handbook" by Vinson Brown, and are reprinted here with the kind permission of the publishers.

Copyright © 1956, 1976 by Vinson Brown

1990 Printing.

ISBN 0-87961-054-9 Paper Edition

Naturegraph Publishers, Inc., Happy Camp, CA

24 Guide to Common Rocks

SPINEL (black, red, violet, blue, green, orange-brown, white)

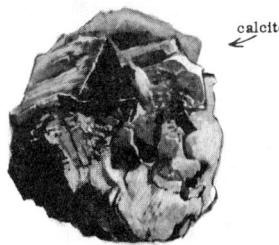

← calcite

transparent to opaque

black (*galinite*), black, yellow or greenish-brown (*picotite*). **Habitat:** often found as twined or simple octahedral crystals in pebbles, solid rock, or as loose grains, particularly in basic igneous rocks such as gabbro or basalt; also found in metamorphic rocks such as gneiss, granular limestone, and serpentine.

3. **ANDALUSITE.** *Hardness* 7.5; *sp. gr.* 3.1-3.2; *cleavage* imperfect and prismatic. **Habitat:** often found as rough, large and nearly square reddish or gray crystals of prismatic shape, showing symmetrically arranged dark and light areas in cross section; or more rarely as granular or columnar very tough masses; usually among metamorphic rocks such as slates, schists or gneisses; rarely in granites.

ANDALUSITE (pink, brown, gray, white)

often symetrically arranged black areas

coarse irregular crystals

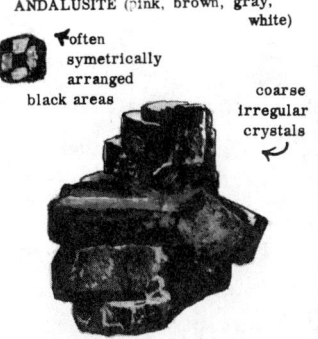

TOURMALINE (black, white, pink, red, blue, green, brown and colorless) colors often zoned

4. **TOURMALINE**. *Hardness* 7-7.5; *sp. gr.* 2.2-3.2; *fracture* conchoidal to irregular. **Habitat:** found often as slender prismatic crystals with triangular cross sections,

Rock Forming Minerals 23

Color: Most minerals, and almost all rocks, occur in so many different colors that color is not a good physical test. However, certain minerals tend to be light colored and others dark, and there are a few minerals, such as **lepidolite**, (usually lilac), that have distinctive common colors.

Crystals: Many minerals form into *crystals* of distinctive appearance. Some of these are shown in the mineral illustrations and will help in identification; but most rock-forming minerals will be found in *massive* and other *noncrystalline* forms.

All the minerals discussed below are arranged in descending order of hardness.

1. **TOPAZ.** *Hardness* 8; *sp. gr.* 3.4-3.6; *color* (see accompanying picture); *fracture* conchoidal to uneven; *cleavage* perfect or basal. **Habitat:** found as crystals in water-worn and rounded pebbles in placer deposits, also in pegmatitic cavities and in strongly acid igneous rocks such as rhyolites and granites.

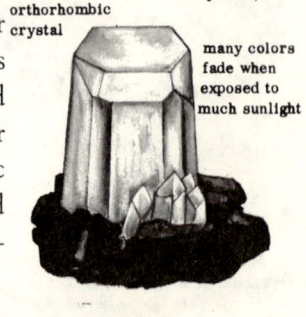

TOPAZ (colorless, pink, blue yellow)
orthorhombic crystal
many colors fade when exposed to much sunlight

2. **SPINEL.** *Hardness* 7.5-8; *sp. gr.* 3.5-4.5; *cleavage* imperfect and octahedral; *color* deep red (*ruby spinel*), yellow or orange-red (*rubicelle*), blue to light blue (*blue spinel*), green, brown or

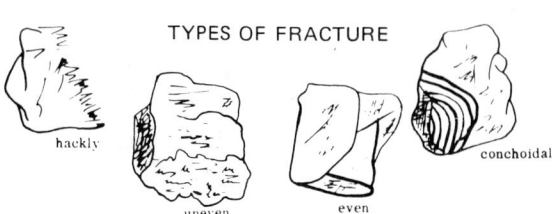

TYPES OF FRACTURE — hackly, uneven, even, conchoidal

Fracture: When a mineral breaks into irregular sections instead of smooth planes, it is said to *fracture*. Four common types of fracture are shown in the picture above.

Luster: How light reflects from the surface of a mineral determines its type of *luster*. In minerals the main division is into *metallic* or *nonmetallic* luster. Most rock-forming minerals have various kinds of nonmetallic luster, such as glassy (vitreous), adamantine (diamond sparkling), pearly, resinous (like tree resin), silky, greasy, earthy, and waxy or soap-like. The minerals described in this book may be presumed to have a *glassy* luster unless other forms of luster are mentioned.

Streak: When a mineral is rubbed hard, especially a sharp point, on a piece of unglazed porcelain (as shown), it forms a powdery *streak*, and this streak may be different from its normal color, sometimes being very distinctive for a particular mineral. If the streak is *white* it is not mentioned in the mineral descriptions.

Rock Forming Minerals 21

has a hook at one end to which you can tie your specimen. Weigh your mineral first in air, and then in water. Subtract the weight in water from the weight in air; then divide this *difference* between the two weights *into* the weight in air. In the example shown in the illustration, 4.1 grams is subtracted from 5.2 grams, which = 1.1. This, divided into 5.2, gives a specific gravity of 4.73, which would fit most closely the mineral pyrrhotite, which has a specific gravity of 4.7. A little less heavy would be the mineral barite with a sp. gr. of 4.5. It is important of course to have enough of a specific mineral to be *able* to weigh it.

Cleavage: When struck, most minerals break in certain definite directions. We call this *cleavage*. The usually smooth surfaces left by this breaking are called cleavage *planes*, which are also the planes of the crystal structure and so are parallel to the possible crystal *faces*. The exact angle and type of cleavage is often important in identification. Six common types of cleavage are shown in the illustration.

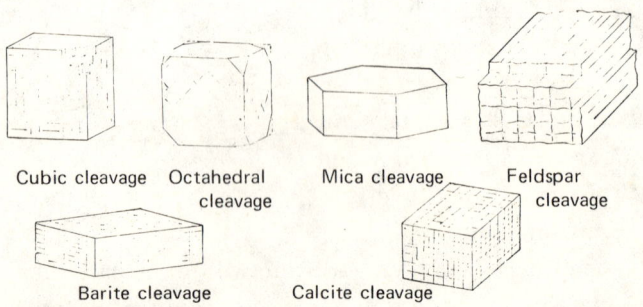

Cubic cleavage Octahedral cleavage Mica cleavage Feldspar cleavage

Barite cleavage Calcite cleavage

20 Guide to Common Rocks

One particular reason for learning these rock-forming minerals and the chart of their rock associations on page 54 is to be able to name a certain kind of rock by its dominant mineral. Thus, schists are called **mica** schist, **tremolite** schist, **chromite** schist, and so on, as the result of noticing which particular type of mineral is found in each. There are also other shades of meaning, as when a common kind of limestone is always assumed to be mainly a **calcite** limestone, but a harder kind of limestone is called a **dolomitic** limestone because it is dominated by a harder kind of calcium/magnesium carbonate mineral called **dolomite**. To determine the particular kind of mineral that is dominant in a rock, you need to study carefully the mineral descriptions given below, and be able to identify them by their special qualities whenever encountered.

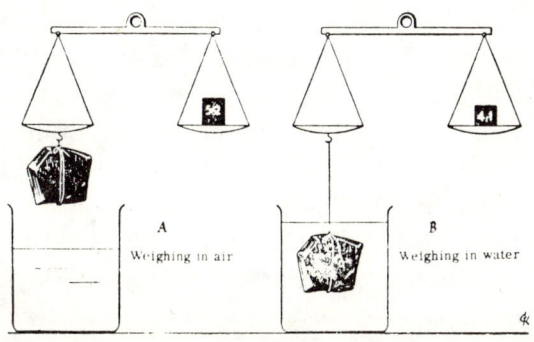

A Weighing in air
B Weighing in water

Specific gravity is a quality found in each mineral, and may be almost as important as hardness. To find specific gravity the simplest way is to get a little hand-held spring scale (very cheap) that

ROCK FORMING MINERALS

It is important to know the minerals that form rocks because many rocks can be identified by name only when you know something about the minerals that form rocks. These minerals are by far the most plentiful on earth. In this book we have arranged their descriptions by order of hardness, with the hardest mineral first, so that as you test these minerals you will start with the hardness test.

Hardness of minerals is based on the following scale, called Moh's Scale, in which the minerals in **bold** type are easy to find and use for testing hardness.

1. **Talc** (extremely soft)
2. **Gypsum** (soft)
3. **Calcite** (hard like c.p.)*
4. Fluorite
5. Apatite
6. **Feldspar** (orthoclase)
7. **Quartz**
8. **Topaz**
9. Corundum
10. Diamond (hardest)

Diamond is so extremely hard (especially on its octahedral or cleavage face) that there is more difference in hardness between it and corundum than there is between corundum and talc! So this scale is not an evenly spaced scale of hardness, but only relative. Usually in testing hardness we use a fingernail to find a hardness of 2.5, a copper coin to show a hardness of 3, a knife to test a hardness of 5.5, and a sharp piece of quartz to give a hardness of 7. Each can scratch any mineral softer than itself.

* c.p. = copper penny

Rock Forming Minerals 25

or in radiating crystalline masses or aggregates; found often in pegmatites, but also in metamorphic rocks such as crystalline limestones, schists, and gneisses; often as small round grains in sand or sandstones.

5. **GARNET.** *Hardness* 6.5-7.5; *sp. gr.* 3.4-4.3; *fracture* even; *colors* many, but most common are reddish brown or dark red. **Habitat:** often found as small cube-shaped crystals, round glassy grains, or granular, laminated or compact massive aggregates. Abundant in crystalline gneisses and schists, crystalline limestones, peridotites and serpentines, and in many igneous rocks; frequent as round grains in sand.

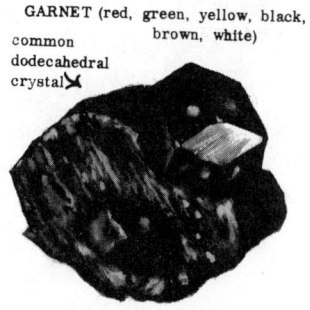

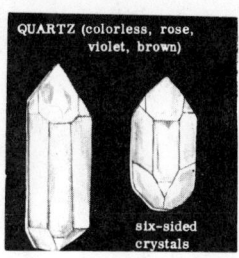

6. **QUARTZ.** *Hardness* 7; *sp. gr.* 2.6-2.7; *fracture* conchoidal. **Habitat:** usually found in massive forms, or grains (as in sand), but occasionally in beautiful 6-sided crystals, as shown, or as one the major components of granite and other igneous rocks; often found as beach or stream pebbles, and is mined from pegmatite dikes and quartz veins in solid rock. Many colors.

Varieties of *quartz* include: *rock crystal*, transparent quartz crystals; *smoky quartz* or *cairngorm*, smoke-colored; *amethyst*, a purple or violet variety of quartz used in jewelry; *citrine quartz*, yellow colored; *rose quartz*, pale red and massive; *milky quartz*, white opaque to translucent; *cat's eye*, greenish, grayish or brownish, and opalescent because of other mineral fibers; *iron* or *ferruginous quartz*, brownish or reddish-brown and opaque; and others.

Chalcedony is a kind of reformed quartz, which is transparent to translucent to opaque, but has a greasy luster and occurs in many colors. *Agate* is a banded and varicolored form of chalcedony; *onyx* a black-and-white banded form (sometimes other colors in the bands, as brown and white bands in *sardonyx*); *carnelian* or *sard*, a reddish form; *chrysoprase*, an apple green form; *jasper*, an opaque reddish-brown form, often with black intrusions; *flint*, a form with whitish-coated gray, grayish-brown or brownish-black opaque-to-translucent nodules, with excellent conchoidal fracture (thus good for making arrow heads).

7. **OLIVINE.** *Hardness* 6.5-7; *sp. gr.* 3.2-3.6; *color* olive green to grayish or yellowish green, also brown, reddish, yellowish, or colorless; *cleavage* pinacoidal (tablet-like with two parallel axes); *fracture* conchoidal; *soluble* in hydrochloric acid. **Habitat:** usually found in granular aggregates (like granulated sugar) or as small scattered grains, but

Rock Forming Minerals   27

sometimes in masses, mainly identified with granites, or as forsterite olivine in metamorphic limestones, also in serpentine.

8. **KYANITE.** *Hardness* double: 5 parallel to the length of the crystal, and 7 across; *sp. gr.* 3.5-3.7; *cleavage* good in 3 directions. **Habitat:** usually found in slender, blade-like crystals, blue in color, or in radial aggregates or fibrous masses, associated with metamorphic rocks, especially schists and gneisses; more rarely in granite.

KYANITE (greenish, bluish, to colorless)

bladed crystal in quartz

PYRITE (often called fool's gold) (brass yellow, opaque)

Pyrithohedron sometimes

usually striated cubes

9. **PYRITE.** *Hardness* 6-6.5; *sp. gr.* 4.9-5.2; *fracture* uneven; *streak* (when rubbed on unglazed porcelain) greenish to brownish black; *luster* metallic. Called "Fool's Gold" because of brass-yellow or golden color. **Habitat:** found mainly as cubic crystals with striated (grooved) faces, or in crystalline masses, in veins and as nodules, associated with sedimentary or crystalline rocks of many ages.

10. **FELDSPARS.** *Hardness* 6-6.5; *sp. gr.* 2.5-2.6; *cleavage* good in 2 directions nearly at right

angles to each other; *fracture* uneven; *luster* from vitreous (glassy) to pearly or satiny; *plagioclase* feldspars show striations (tiny grooves) on one of the cleavage faces, and are white, tan, or gray; *orthoclase* and *microcline* feldspars lack striations and are generally white, gray, red, or green. **Habitat:** *feldspars* are major components of granitic and other igneous rocks, including pegmatite dikes, associated with quartz and mica.

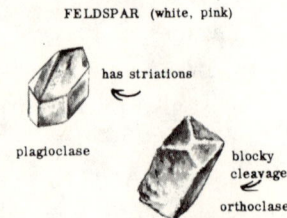

11. **GLAUCOPHANE.** *Hardness* 6-6.5; *sp. gr.* 3.0-3.11; *cleavage* in 2 directions, 56 and 124 degrees; *fracture* conchoidal to uneven; *colors* bluish, bluish black or grayish; *streak* grayish blue. **Habitat:** commonly found as a component of *glaucophane schist* and *gneiss*.

12. **OPAL.** *Hardness* 5.5-6.5; *sp. gr.* 2.1-2.3; *fracture* conchoidal to irregular; *luster* glassy, pearly, greasy, or dull, transparent to opaque; opalescent appearance is caused by internal refractions of the light; *color* none (hyaline opal), or almost any color. **Habitat:** often found as veins, seams, or lining the inside of rock cavities; also in kidney-shaped and stalactitic forms; usually in igneous and sedimentary rocks; sometimes replaces wood to produce *opalized wood*.

Rock Forming Minerals 29

13. **AMPHIBOLES.** This is a group of rock-forming minerals having the following common properties; *hardness* 5-6; *sp. gr.* 3-3.3; *luster* glassy or pearly, but silky with fibrous varieties (asbes-

AMPHIBOLE (black, green, white)
luster glassy
good cleavage

tos); *cleavage* in 2 directions, at 56 and 124 degrees; *color* is white to light green in *tremolite*, light green to dark green in *actinolite*, and dark green to black in *hornblende;* *crystals* monoclinic, which means their axes or centers are of unequal length, 2 of which cross each other at an oblique angle, and both of which are perpendicular to the third. **Habitat:** very common as crystals, or components of igneous rocks, though often in other kinds of rocks, too.

PYROXENE (green, black, white, pink, violet)

Diopside

Augite

14. **PYROXENES.** This group of rock-forming minerals has the following common properties: *hardness* 5-6; *sp. gr.* 3.2-3.5; *crystal* a stout prism, as shown; *colors;* the white to deep grass-green form is *diopside;* the violet-colored form is *violan*; the dark-green to black is *augite*, the commonest mineral of the pyroxene group: It is brittle, dark greenish or black, glassy, and sometimes can be scratched with a knife, sometimes not. It is most commonly found as grains in rock and these are very hard to tell apart

from similar hornblende; but use a magnifying glass to notice the occasionally short, blocky crystals and the way augite splits (cleaves) in 2 directions at nearly right angles. **Habitat:** found in stout prismatic crystals (as shown), and as irregular grains, mainly in igneous rocks, *violan* and *augite* in the dark igneous rocks and *diopside* in the light-colored rocks; also in schists and gneisses.

15. **CHROMITE.** *Hardness* 5.5; *sp. gr.* 4.3-4.6; *cleavage* octahedral; *luster* metallic to submetallic or pitch-like; *color* brownish black to iron-black; *streak* brownish black, like coffee. **Habitat:** commonly a component of most basic igneous rocks, such as gabbro, and basalt.

16. **APATITE.** *Hardness* 5; *sp. gr.* 3.1-3.2; *cleavage* imperfect and basal; *fracture* conchoidal; *luster* glassy to greasy; *color* brown, green, yellow, red, gray, violet, or colorless; often with several colors at once, appearing patchy. **Habitat:** commonly found in small amounts in most igneous rocks; often in larger quantities in igneous dikes.

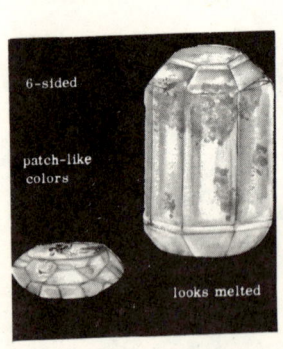

17. **MAGNESITE.** *Hardness* 3.5-4.5; *sp. gr.* 3-3.2; *fracture* conchoidal; *luster* earthy or dull.

Fizzes in hot hydrochloric acid. **Habitat:** a magnesium ore that often appears as white to light-brown veins in serpentine rock. In the old days some California Indians baked magnesite to turn it a beautiful yellow-brown, then ground it into round beads and polished to a fine color to use as money.

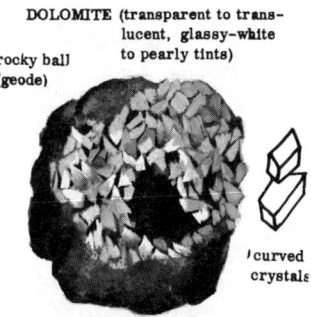

DOLOMITE (transparent to translucent, glassy-white to pearly tints)
rocky ball (geode)
curved crystals

18. **DOLOMITE.** *Hardness* 3.5-4; *sp. gr.* 2.8-2.9; *cleavage* good rhombohedral in crystals; *luster* glassy or pearly in crystals, dull or earthy in finely granular. Fizzes lightly with cold hydrochloric acid along scratch; good fizzing with hot acid. A calcium/magnesium carbonate, closely related to limestone, but harder. **Habitat:** usually occurs as a massive, coarsely to finely granular rock, often in beds associated with limestone and other sedimentary rocks.

19. **ALUNITE** (Alum Stone). *Hardness* 3.5-4; *sp. gr.* 2.58-2.8; *cleavage* perfect basal in crystals; *luster* glassy, but pearly on cleavage edges; *fracture* conchoidal, earthy or splintery; *color* yellowish, white, grayish, reddish, or colorless. **Habitat:** found occasionally as cubic or tabular rhombohedral crystals, but more often as light-colored fibrous or finely granular compact rock, looking like dull limestone; more rarely mixed with siliceous material to

form a compact, granular, hard, nearly white rock, especially among volcanic rocks.

20. **SERPENTINE (ANTIGORITE).** *Hardness* 2.5-4; *sp. gr.* 2.5-2.8; *fracture* conchoidal to splintery; *luster* greasy, waxy, or silky; *color* mainly in shades of greenish to black, but also brownish, yellowish, grayish, and reddish, commonly mottled. A fibrous kind is called *chrysotile*; a massive but impure variety showing mixed lighter veins and patches of calcite, dolomite or magnesite, is called *verde antique*. **Habitat:** *antigorite* is the main component of serpentine rock, which appears often in veins as a metamorphic rock, changed by water from magnesian silicate rocks and minerals such as pyroxene and olivine.

SERPENTINE (green, brown, black, yellow, red, white)
waxy appearance
greasy feel
often banded with asbestos

21. **LEPIDOLITE.** *Hardness* 2-4; *sp. gr.* 2.8-2.9; *cleavage* perfect and basal, cleavage plates usually appearing elastic; *luster* pearly; *color* usually lilac or pink. **Habitat:** commonly found in compact aggregates of tiny scales, forming granular, scaly masses; sometimes in short prismatic crystals; rather rarely in large sheets or plates; associated with pegmatite dikes; also in gneisses, schists, and granites.

Rock Forming Minerals 33

22. **CHRYSOTILE ASBESTOS.** *Hardness* 3-3.5; *sp. gr.* 2.2-2.3; *luster* greasy to subresinous, pearly, and silky; *color* varies from olive-green to yellowish to pink and white. **Habitat:** occurs in aggregates of fine silky fibers, often as long as six inches, or much more, most often brilliant white, and associated with serpentine rock, of which it is the *asbestos* form; also found in altered peridotite rock, and in limestone rock where it is in contact with intrusive sheets or sills of igneous rock.

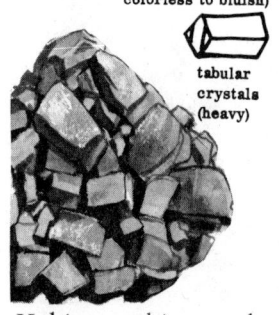

BARITE (glassy, transparent, colorless to bluish)

tabular crystals (heavy)

23. **BARITE.** *Hardness* 2.5-3.5; *sp. gr.* 4.3-4.6; *cleavage* perfect, 2, at right angles; *luster* glassy to pearly or almost resinous, but earthy when granular; *color* white to light shades of gray, yellow, blue, brown, or red. **Habitat:** this very heavy nonmetallic mineral is often found in granular or crystalline nodules or masses, and is usually light in color; found as beds or veins, especially in limestones, dolomites and shales, but also in other sedimentary rocks, as residual nodules left over from the weathering of dolomite and limestone, or as light-colored veins or beds in more important ores.

24. **CALCITE.** *Hardness* 3; *sp. gr.* 2.7; *luster* glassy to earthy or dull; *cleavage* perfect rhombohedral. Fizzes easily with cold dilute acids, a property no other mineral possesses. **Varieties** include:

satin spar calcite, fibrous and with a silky luster; *Iceland spar*, clear as glass; *massive calcite*, marble and limestones; *onyx marble*, a banded form found in cave linings; *stalactites*, icicle-like, hanging from cave roofs; *stalagmites*, the same, rising from cave floors; *travertine*, banded formations found around springs and stream beds; *calcareous tufa* and *sinter*, porous formations about calcareous mineral springs. **Other habitats:** found as the major constituent of limestone and marble; also mixed with other sedimentary rocks.

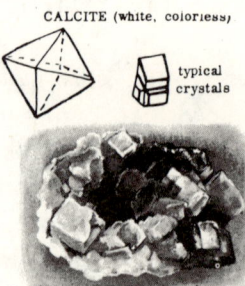

25. **MICA.** *Hardness* 2-3; *sp. gr.* 2.75-3; *cleavage* perfect basal, producing very thin, usually elastic, tough plates; *luster* glassy to pearly. Common kinds include: *muscovite*, the common light-colored mica (light brown, or clear); *biotite*, dark-brown to black; *mariposite*, apple green; *lepidolite*, lilac, lavender, violet-blue pink and, rarely, colorless. Often in scaly masses; fuses in flame to bubbly transparent glass. **Habitat:** common in granites and schists.

Rock Forming Minerals 35

26. **CHLORITE.** *Hardness* 2-2.5; *sp. gr.* 2.6-2.9; *luster* pearly; *cleavage*, the same as in mica (see 25), but the plates are brittle and not elastic. *Color* green; rarely white, pale yellow, or rose red; usually opaque, very rarely translucent or transparent. **Habitat:** commonly found as *chlorite schist*.

27. **SALT (HALITE).** *Hardness* 2-2.5; *sp. gr.* 2.1-2.6; *taste* salty, (soluble in water); *cleavage* very good cubical; *fracture* conchoidal; *color* white, colorless, gray, yellow, brown, blue, or reddish. **Habitat:** rarely found in pure state, but commonly mixed with other salts, often with gypsum, anhydrite, clay, organic matter, and so on; *rock salt* may form extensive deposits, made from ancient seas, associated with sedimentary rock beds; sometimes found around volcanoes, also as foam-like earthy crusts in dry lake beds and similar arid places.

28. **GYPSUM.** *Hardness* 1.5-2.5; *sp. gr.* 2.3; *cleavage* in its selenite (clear) form perfect in one plane, but fibrous in a second direction at angles of 66 and 114 degrees;

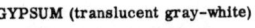
GYPSUM (translucent gray-white)
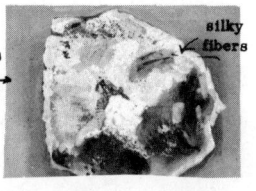
white patches of powder →
silky fibers

fracture in massive kinds is uneven; when heated to about 400 degrees F., it turns dense white in color, peels off in flakes, and fuses into round globules, which can be crushed to make plaster of Paris; *color* white or colorless in pure forms, but otherwise gray to black, yellow or blue, and light pink to red and brown. **Habitat:** *rock gypsum* commonly is found in beds with sedimentary rocks; earthy gypsum (*gypsite*) forms surface beds. Transparent forms are *selenite*, snowy-white is *alabaster*, and silky is *satin spar*.

29. **SULFUR.** *Hardness* 1.5-2.5; *sp. gr.* 1.9-2.1; *melting point* very low, 110-119 degrees C; *ignites* easily at 248 degrees C; *fracture* conchoidal to uneven. **Habitat:** common in sedimentary rock beds with gypsum, limestone, anhydrite, and various hydrocarbons, sulfates and carbonates; often found in deposits around hot springs.

30. **DIATOMITE** (also called **Diatomaceous Earth**). *Hardness* 1-1.5; *sp. gr.* when pure and dry 0.45 (floats in water), but up to 2.1-2.2 with water content; *luster* dull and earthy; *soluble* in alkalies, but insoluble in acids; *color* commonly pure white, cream or gray, but also pinkish to reddish and brownish. **Habitat:** usually found in beds in sedimentary rocks, varying in texture from loose to compact grains in a porous aggregate.

NAMING YOUR ROCKS

To help you identify and collect rocks you need the following tools: (1) a hammer or a geologic pick, (2) a cold chisel, (3) a cloth bag or knapsack for collecting, (4) some numbers written on adhesive tape and this stuck to a piece of wax paper, (5) a bottle of dilute hydrochloric acid, (6) a magnifying glass, (7) a knife, and (8) a copper coin. As you collect rocks, put a number on each one with the adhesive tape, and write in a small notebook, after the number, the name of the locality where you found the rock. Wrap the more delicate rocks in newspaper to protect them from harm.

The rocks described in the next pages are divided into the following main divisions:

A. **Fine-grained or glassy rocks**, p. 38.
   1. Glassy igneous rocks, p. 39.
   2. Small-grained rocks, p. 40.

B. **Rocks with visible grains or crystals**, p. 48.
   1. Cemented rocks with visible grains, p. 49.
   2. Large-grained metamorphic and igneous rocks with fused grains or crystals, p. 50.

When you start to identify your rock, break it through the middle so that you can find a fresh surface. Examine this surface carefully, first with your eyes and then with a magnifying glass.

If the rock has many visible grains on its surface and these are either tightly packed crystals (igneous or metamorphic rocks), or grains of gravel, sand or other rock pieces cemented together (sedimentary rocks), then turn to B. on page 48. (**Note:** rocks may be either fine or coarse of grain, or may be lumpy with pebbles of many sizes, but no magnifying glass is needed to see grains.)

If the rock is without visible grains on its surface or only a few scattered ones, then study the rock descriptions given in A. below. (The appearance of the surface may be glass-like or soap-like, or so very fine-grained that the individual grains can be seen only under a magnifying glass. The rock may be very solid (compact) or it may be full of small holes (porous or cellular), or it may turn to powder on rubbing between the fingers.)

A. FINE-GRAINED OR GLASSY ROCKS

If the rock is usually glasslike or pitchlike and either full of holes (frothy) or solid (and then not scratched with a knife), see 1. on page 39.

If the rock is generally dull (not like glass), though sometimes shiny if worn smooth by water and slick or greasy if green, and with tiny grains of crystals seen in the magnifying glass, see 2. on p. 40.

1. GLASSY IGNEOUS ROCKS

These rocks appear like glass because the red-hot liquid lava from which they came cooled too rapidly to form any crystals.

Glasslike igneous rocks are divided into two main kinds: those which are solid, of medium weight and cannot be scratched with a knife, and those which are frothy or full of holes, very light-weight rocks and usually scratched with a knife.

The frothy or hole-filled rocks are generally gray to whitish in color, and either dull glassy or with a sheen like silk. If the holes are small with thin walls, the rock is a **pumice**; if holes are large and thick-walled, a **scoria** (see p. 42).

Formerly frothy or porous rocks whose holes have become filled with light or dark material by deposition of minerals from liquids appear to be dotted with round spots, either light colored on dark rocks or dark colored on light-colored rocks. These rocks are called **amygdaloids**.

The solid glassy rocks are often colored black or dark brown, dark gray or reddish (rarely green), and they break into shell-like or curved (conchoidal) pieces. They cannot be scratched with a knife, and are very

OBSIDIAN (natural glass)

mottled color

glassy in appearance. If no crystals are visible, it is an **obsidian** rock. If a few visible crystals are embedded in the glass it is **vitrophyre** or **obsidian porphyry**.

Perlite is a grayish variety of obsidian, which shows circular, shelly rings due to curved cracks produced by contraction in cooling. It has a waxy to pearly luster and a splintery fracture.

2. SMALL-GRAINED ROCKS

These rocks appear grained, but the grains can usually be seen clearly only under a magnifying glass, except for occasional scattered large crystals (porphyritic rocks). **Note: chert** (see page 14) may seem so fine-grained as to appear almost glassy, like obsidian, but chert is duller and does not usually break into very good curved chips.

Put a drop of hydrochloric acid on the rock and see if it fizzes along a scratch. Touch the rock in several places with the acid and make sure the fizzing is not caused by just a thin surface layer or a vein in the rock. If the rock does fizz on its main part or along a scratch, turn to b. on page 47. If the rock does not fizz, see a. below.

a. *Rock does not fizz with acid.*

Try scratching the rock with a knife. If it is hard to scratch on its *firm* surface (not where it is full of small holes or cells), then turn to (2) on page 45. But if the rock is easy to scratch with a knife, look to (1) below.

(1) Soft, small-grained rocks.

If the rock powders easily between the fingers or has a gritty feel and is colored white or whitish, it is either **diatomite**, which absorbs water very quickly and powders finely, **chalk**, which powders finely, but does not absorb water quickly, or **tuff**, which sponges up water slowly, does not powder finely, and has a gritty feel.

If the rock does not powder easily between the fingers, but leaves a black mark on the hand, it is one of the varieties of **coal**. With greater decomposition and increasing pressure the softer types change gradually into the harder types of coal. **Peat** is spongy and brown (made of partly decayed and hardened plant material); **lignite** looks like a brownish-black piece of wood, but it splits into bedding planes; **bituminous** is a brittle black and breaks into cubes; while **anthracite** is a dense, glassy black, breaking unevenly.

If the rock does not powder easily nor give a gritty feel and leaves no black mark on the hands, study the rock descriptions below.

If the rock appears in layers which can be split apart, turn to (b) on p. 43.

If the rock does not show layers or cannot be split into layers, then it is described under (a) below.

(a) Unlayered rocks.

If the rock is full of holes, tiny or large, is grayish to whitish in color, and is light in weight, then it is either a **scoria** (large holes), or a **pumice** (tiny and thin-walled holes) which floats in water. Pumice is produced by volcanic eruptions of silicic foam glass.

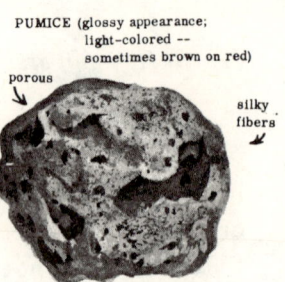

PUMICE (glossy appearance; light-colored -- sometimes brown on red)
porous
silky fibers
will float

If the rock is black, purplish or dark gray, has only a few holes and is of medium weight, it is **basalt**. Rarely reddish in color. (See page 47.)

If the rock has no holes, see descriptions below.

If at least part of the surface of the rock feels waxy or slick, then either it is **serpentine**, which cannot be scratched by the fingernail, or it is **steatite (soapstone)**, which the fingernail can scratch.

Serpentine is usually dark greenish-gray or greenish in color, with the weathered surfaces sometimes rusty, often mottled whitish or with greenish-white veins. It is more rarely blackish, grayish or even multicolored. It may be waxy, greasy or dull in appearance, with a smooth-to-greasy feel.

Naming Your Rocks 43

Steatite or **soapstone** is usually white or gray in color. The Indians carved bowls out of it.

If the surface of the rock is not waxy or slick, but usually gritty or smooth and often with a clayey odor when wet, then it is either **shale** or **tuff**. Shales which do not split are usually called by the name **mudstone**. (See full descriptions of both shale and tuff below.)

Phosphate rock *(phosphorite)* appears in various forms, from an earthy, granular, loosely gathered-together mass to a rock of hardness 2-5. Color may be gray, brown, bluish-gray, black, or white. Phosphorite is a calcium carbonate/phosphate, usually originating through the phosphorylation of limestone.

(b) Layered rocks.

If the rock breaks into slabs with flat or curving and shell-like surface or into sharp chips, turn to **shale** and **tuff** below. Both usually have clayey odor and may contain various fossils.

If the rock splits into thin slabs (like the slate on a blackboard) or into thicker slabs with very flat surfaces which are not easily scratched with a knife, and which have a shiny surface, then it

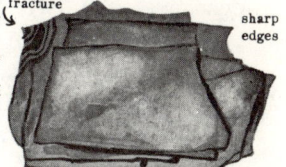

SLATE (dark gray to black, some red, green, purple and brown variations)
conchoidal fracture
sharp edges
often fine mica flakes

is **slate**. The color is usually gray or black, but may be brown, yellowish-brown, greenish, reddish or purplish. The surface is often banded with various colors. No fossils.

If the rock breaks into thickly irregular slabs, usually the blue color of *glaucophane*, it is **glaucophane (amphibole schist)**.

Tuff *is a rock which usually breaks up into sharp chips with smooth fracture,* and these, when ground up, have a gritty feel. When moistened, it may give a slight odor of clay. Color is whitish, light gray, pinkish, yellowish or other light color. Tiny glass shards usually are visible under the magnifying glass. Tuff comes from volcanic ash, but admixed mud or other sediment makes tuffs grade gradually into shales.

Shale usually breaks into shell-like or curved chips (conchoidal fracture), and when ground into dust it is usually smooth and not gritty. If moistened, it generally smells strongly of clay.

SHALE (black, white, dark greens and reds)

thin layers, clay particles & little sand

conchoidal (shell-like) fracture

Shale is a mixture of so many substances that there is a wide variation in color, composition and appearance. Mudstone does not split; sandy shale has much sand; limy shale has some calcite in it from seashells, and fizzes when touched with hydrochloric acid. White, hard and gritty shales are usually made partly of volcanic ash (so are partly tuff).

(2) Very hard, small-grained rocks.

If the rock has large scattered crystals embedded in its surface, it is a **porphyry** (see p. 51).

The following rocks are without such crystals.

(a) Rocks in bands or in layers.

If the rock has no obvious bands, but is in parallel layers of different texture that can be broken apart into approximately rectangular pieces, then it is **cherty shale**. It has hard silica layers.

If the rock has colored bands, it is one of the six rocks described below.

Cherty diatomite has white, soft, chalky layers between dark, hard layers. It absorbs water easily.

Rhyolite often shows flow bands of lava in different colors (see **dacite** color plate on back cover), and is light-colored. (See also page 46.)

Rocks with darker and lighter stripes, but all of the same hardness are either **quartzite** (p. 51), **slate** (p. 44), **felsite** (p. 46), or **travertine**, which is found around geysers or springs.

(b) Rocks without bands or layers

Chert *is a very hard, noncrystalline, silica rock which shows no tiny holes or pores under the magnifying glass.* It is usually brittle with a slightly

46   Guide to Common Rocks

curved or shell-like fracture; commonly reddish or yellow-brown in color, but often greenish and sometimes black or white; often criss-crossed with white quartz veins. It is common in hard, water-worn pebbles, and in limestone beds. (See also pages 40 and 45 and color plate on back cover.)

If the rock shows tiny holes or pores or is not brittle nor productive of curved chips when broken, see the rock descriptions that follow:

If the rock is light-colored, and usually gray, white, yellowish-brown, cream, pink, greenish or purplish, and sometimes with a few white or dark red bands or lines visible (caused by lava flow), then it is a **felsite** and one of the three kinds of felsitic rocks described below. (See back cover.) Freshly-broken chips of these rocks show white or semitransparent edges.

Rhyolite often has visible *quartz* crystals or grains, and may appear almost as glassy as obsidian, or very fine-textured. Its *orthoclase* feldspar shows no striations, but often shows flowing lines.

RHYOLITE (a felsite)

veins of color ← → often porous

↙ generally banded
May be several colors, but all light of tone

Andesite shows no sign of quartz; otherwise it is very similar to rhyolite, except that its *plagioclase* feldspar has striations on some cleavage faces.

Naming Your Rocks   47

Dacite also shows under the magnifying glass the striations (or tiny grooves) of *plagioclase* feldspar; but unlike **andesite** it contains *quartz* crystals.

(**Note:** felsitic rocks such as **rhyolite** and **andesite** show so many different colors and textures they may be mistaken for **basalt** (see below) when very dark, or **chert** (p. 45) when very fine-grained, or **tuff** (p. 44), or fine-grained **quartzite** (p. 51).

If the rock is dark-colored, it is **basalt**.

BASALT (mostly dark)

usually porous

often has green inclusions of olivine

Basalt is usually black, purplish, dark rusty or dark greenish gray; it is always heavy and often with round gas holes in it. It is the world's most common lava rock, often forming great lava plateaus. It varies from the **aphanitic** type, in which the grains are just barely visible, to **scoria** type in which there are numerous round gas holes, and to **amygdaloidal** basalt where the round holes are filled with mineral. Basalt **porphyry** has angular crystals (see p. 51).

b. Rock fizzes with acid.

If the rock is easily powdered and also can be scratched by a fingernail, either it is **marl**, which has a gray color and clayey odor when wet, or it is **chalk**, which is white and has no clayey odor.

48 Guide to Common Rocks

LIMESTONE (white and many colors) Often found in caves, quarries. Fizzing under acid is best test.

Limestone is a firm rock that does not easily crumble, though it sometimes is easily scratched with a knife. It is colored whitish, gray, brownish, yellowish or black, and may hold crystals or parts of shells. In pure form it is fairly hard, (scratched only with great difficulty by a penny), but it may be mixed with impurities such as clay (clayey limestone) or sand (sandy limestone), which make it softer, or it may be mixed with silica to make it harder, so it is hard to scratch with a knife. If formed in crystal bands or patterns by hot water deposits, it is called **travertine.**

B. ROCKS WITH VISIBLE GRAINS OR CRYSTALS

If all the rock is made up of visible crystals or mineral grains of one or several kinds which give some sparkle in bright light, turn to 2. on page 50.

If the rock is made of rock fragments (including pebbles), or sand or gravel cemented together, it is described under 1. below. (**Note:** if the cemented sand breaks *around* the grains, it is *sandstone*; if it breaks *through* the grains, then it is a *quartzite*, which is described in the Metamorphic Rock section on page 51.)

1. Cemented rocks with visible grains

These are sedimentary rocks made up of either gravel or sand or other rock particles cemented together, often containing fossils and rarely a few scattered crystals. Cement of calcite, clay, etc.

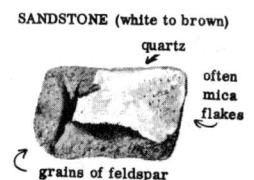

SANDSTONE (white to brown)
quartz
often mica flakes
grains of feldspar

Split slabs = <u>flagstone</u>
Slabs containing much reddish feldspar = <u>brownstone</u>.

Sandstone *is coarse or fine sand cemented together more or less firmly.* It varies greatly, from yellowish-brown to brown, red, yellow, gray or whitish, and may hold shells or other fossils and scattered crystals. Magnifying glass shows rounded and angular grains of quartz and other minerals. Varies greatly in texture: dark gray, **graywacke**; acid-fizzing, **limy sandstone**; very fine-grained, **clayey sandstone**.

Agglomerate is made of volcanic *ash* and angular fragments cemented together. Light colors.

Conglomerate is made of *rounded* pebbles cemented in sand and clay.

Breccia is a cemented aggregate of *angular* fragments of rock of either sedimentary or igneous origin.

CONGLOMERATE ("Puddingstone", variable color)

Rounded pebbles often quartz

sand and gravel → composition

2. Large-grained metamorphic and igneous rocks.

If the rock does not appear banded nor layered, and crystals are rarely flattened, needle-like, or like fused sand grains, turn to b. on page 51.

If the rock appears banded (with darker and lighter lines), or with irregular layers, or the crystals, when magnified, look mainly flattened, needle-like, or like fused sand, see a. below:

a. Banded, crystallized or schistose rocks with visible crystals or grains.

These are crystalline, metamorphic rocks that have been changed from other rocks by heat, etc.

Marble fizzes or foams when touched with acid, especially along a scratch. Has one color, or crudely colored bands.

MARBLE (white, gray)
often banded with impurities
calcite or dolomite crystals sparkle

SCHIST (variable in color)
mica flakes common
fine layered

Mica schist does not fizz, *is not banded*, and is thickly layered with numerous, shiny, silvery flakes of mica. **Chlorite** schist is light green; **talc** schist is whitish and powdery; **garnet** schist is reddish; **glaucophane** schist is blue; **hornblende** schist has dark fibers.

Naming Your Rocks 51

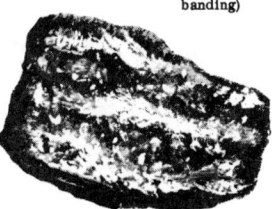
GNEISS (variable color, coarse banding)

Gneiss is a rock made of many kinds of minerals, including rough layers or bands of mica between layers of quartz and feldspar.

Quartzite is a rock made mainly of quartz sand grains so fused together that they break *through the grains* when the rock is fractured (some mica is visible, but not in bands). It cannot be scratched with a knife, and the color varies through whitish, reddish, brownish to greenish, or rarely black.

b. Large-grained igneous rocks.

These rocks have easily visible crystals, tightly packed together, but not flattened, and rarely rounded as in above rocks.

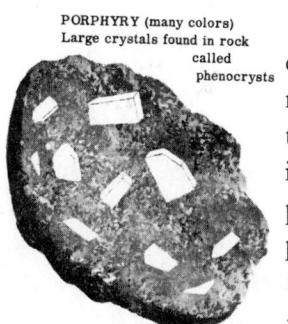
PORPHYRY (many colors)
Large crystals found in rock called phenocrysts

If the rock has large crystals scattered among more numerous small crystals, it is a **Porphyry**, which includes **basalt** porphyry (see p. 47), **felsite** porphyry (see p. 46), **granite** porphyry (p. 52), **obsidian** porphyry (p. 40), and so forth.

If the rock crystals are all of about the same size, see rocks described on the next page.

Gabbro is a rock having approximately 75% dark minerals and 25% light minerals: with square, chunky, dark-green grains of augite (see p. 29). Quartz is generally absent, and the feldspar is often a dark variety, though showing typical feldspar cleavage in 2 directions at nearly right angles, as seen under a magnifying glass. (See color plate on back of cover.)

Diorite is a coarse-grained igneous rock made up of approximately 50% light minerals and 50% dark minerals; quartz is absent. Both (*plagioclase*) feldspars are whitish, never reddish as in granite, and some show striations (small grooves) on the cleavage faces.

Syenite is another, similar, coarse-grained or granitoid igneous rock of about equally mixed light and dark minerals, also without visible quartz, but the whitish (*orthoclase*) feldspar has no striations on any cleavage face. **Syenite** shows less mottling than either granite or diorite.

GRANITE (mottled appearance)
composition of feldspar, quartz,
mica, hornblende, etc.

mica flakes
often present

light weight

Granite is a rock made up of approximately 75% light minerals and 25% dark minerals. The feldspar is pinkish or milky (and appears in ⬜ cleavage blocks); crystals of quartz are glassy white; and there are slender and dark crystals of hornblende or flaky dark crystals of mica. (Back cover.)

Pegmatite is a rock very similar to granite, but with all crystals *very large*. It is found in dikes (see illus. page 8) and in large veins, often with beautiful gem minerals and other rarities (see inside back cover).

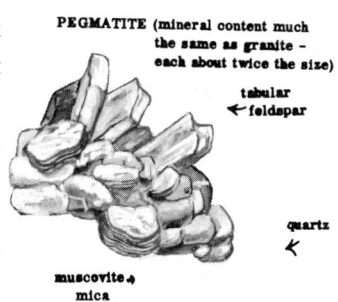

Monzonite has no quartz, but about equal amounts of orthoclase and plagioclase (striated) feldspar. This is a light-colored rock.

Peridotite is a dark greenish-gray or almost black rock, with some shiny or even greasy spots caused by serpentine (see inside back cover). It is an olivine-rich rock, which turns into a blue clay, similar to the famous diamond clay. It usually has plenty of dark greenish augite or other pyroxene minerals and olivine, but little or no feldspar. It is usually the darkest of all igneous rocks.

CHART OF MINERALS ASSOCIATED WITH VARIOUS ROCKS

(Use this chart to determine which kinds of minerals you are most likely to find with each kind of rock. Most important minerals are shown in *italics*.)

SEDIMENTARY: *calcite*, diatomite, *feldspars*, gypsum, opal, pyrite, *quartz*, salt, sulfur, etc.

- **chert:** a smooth, very fine-grained siliceous rock solidified from a hydrated silica gel.
- **conglomerate:** mixed and cemented *pebbles* of quartz, feldspar, chert, etc.
- **limestone:** barite, *calcite*, dolomite, opal, spinel.
- **sandstones:** *augite, feldspars, hornblende,* opal, *quartz,* tourmaline, garnet.
- **shales:** barite, clay minerals (usually silicates).

METAMORPHIC

- **gneiss:** andalusite, *biotite, feldspars,* garnet, *glaucophane,* kyanite, *muscovite, quartz,* spinel, tourmaline.
- **marble (crystalline limestone):** *calcite,* chrysotile asbestos, garnet, olivine, pyrite, tourmaline.
- **petrified wood:** *calcite, agate,* opal.
- **quartzite:** a sandstone (see Sedimentary) strongly cemented by silica.
- **schist:** andalusite, *biotite, chlorite,* garnet, *glaucophane,* kyanite, *muscovite,* tourmaline.

serpentine: *antigorite,* chrysotile asbestos, magnesite, magnetite, olivine, spinel.
slate: andalusite, asbestos, barite, calcite, *clay minerals* (silicates).

IGNEOUS: apatite, feldspar, hornblende, quartz.

GRANULAR IGNEOUS ROCKS

diorite: *diopside, hornblende, plagioclase feldspar,* pyrite.
gabbro: *augite,* chromite, hornblende, *plagioclase feldspar,* pyrite, spinel, violan.
granite: *biotite, feldspar,* garnet, hornblende, kyanite, *muscovite, olivine,* pyrite, *quartz,* topaz.
peridotite: *augite,* chrysotile asbestos, garnet, *hornblende, olivine.*

FINE-GRAINED IGNEOUS ROCKS

andesite: *augite, diopside, plagioclase feldspar.*
basalt: *augite,* chromite, *olivine, plagioclase feldspar,* spinel.
rhyolite: *feldspars, hornblende, quartz,* topaz.
syenite: biotite, hornblende, *microcline* and *orthoclase feldspars,* pyroxene, zircon.

GLASSY IGNEOUS ROCKS

basaltic glass: *augite,* chromite, *hornblende, plagioclase feldspar,* pyrite, spinel, violan.
obsidian: *biotite mica, feldspars, hornblende, quartz.*

pitchstone: same as obsidian, but has more water in composition, and is more resinous and pitch-like; sometimes has alunite.

pumice: same minerals as obsidian, but filled with air voids.

PORPHYRYTIC IGNEOUS ROCKS

andesite porphyry: same minerals as andesite.
basalt porphyry: same minerals as basalt.
felsite porphyry: same minerals as granite or obsidian.

INDEX

Acid, 11,23,50
Actinolite, 29
Adamantine, 22
Agate, 26,54
Agglomerate, 49
Aggregate, 25
Alabaster, 36
Alum, 31
Aluminum, 17
Alunite, 31,56
Amber, 15
Amethyst, 26
Amphibole, 29,44
Amygdaloid, 39,47
Andalusite, 24,54,55
Andesite, 46,47,55,56
Anhydrite, 14
Anthracite, 41
Antigorite, 32
Apatite, 19,30,55
Aphanitic, 47
Asbestos, 29,33,54,55
Ash, 44,49
Augite, 11,29,52,54,55

Banded, 50
Barite, 21,33,54,55
Basalt, 42,47,51,55,56
Basic, 11
Batholith, 9
Biotite, 11,34,54,55
Bituminous, 41
Breccia, 49

Cairngorm, 26
Calcite, 14,19,20,33,54,55
Calcium, 14
Carbonate, 14

Carnelian, 26
Cat's eye, 26
Chalcedony, 26
Chalk, 14,41,47
Chert, 14,15,40,45,47,54
Chlorite, 35,50,54
Chromite, 20,30,55
Chrysoprase, 26
Chrysotile, 32,33,54,55
Citrine, 26
Clay, 44,54,55
Cleavage, 19,21
Coal, 15,41
Color, 23
Compound, 9
Conchoidal, 24,26
Conglomerate, 13,49,54
Coquina, 15
Coral, 14
Corundum, 19
Crystal, 11,15,23,37,48,
 50,51,53

Dacite, 45,47
Diamond, 19,22
Diatomaceous earth, 36
Diatomite, 15,36,41,45,48,54
Dike, 10,53
Diopside, 29,55
Diorite, 8,52,55
Dolomite, 14,20,31

Earthy, 22
Element, 9
Extrusion, 9,10

Face, 19,21
Feldspar, 8,9,11,17,19,27,
 51,52,54,55

Felsite, 45,46,51,56
First rocks, 9
Flint, 26
Fluorite, 19
Fool's Gold, 27
Forsterite, 27
Fossil, 11
Fracture, 22

Gabbro, 24,52,55
Gahnite, 24
Garnet, 17,25,50,54,55
Glassy, 22,37,39,55
Glaucophane, 17,28,44,50,54
Gneiss, 17,51,54
Grain, 37,38,40,48,50,51
Granite, 9,51,52,55,56
Graywacke, 49
Greasy, 22
Gypsum, 14,19,35,54

Habitat, 23
Halite, 35
Hardness, 19,20
Hornblende, 9,11,29,50,54,55
Hydrochloric acid, 31,37,40

Iceland spar, 34
Igneous, 9,11
Intermediate, 11
Intrusion, 9,10
Iron, 9,14,26

Jasper, 26

Kaolin, 17
Kyanite, 27,54,55

Laccolith, 10

Lava, 10,39
Lepidolite, 23,32,34
Lignite, 41
Limestone, 14,48,54
Luster, 22

Magma, 9,10,15
Magnesite, 30,55
Magnesium, 14,31
Magnetite, 55
Marble, 50,54
Mariposite, 34
Marl, 47
Massive, 23
Mechanical, 13
Metallic, 22
Metamorphic, 9,15,54
Mica, 9,11,15,20,34,51,55
Microcline, 28,55
Mineral, 9,54,56
Moh's Scale, 19
Monoclinic, 29
Monzonite, 53
Mudstone, 43,44
Muscovite, 34,54,55

Nodule, 27
Noncrystalline, 23
Nonmetallic, 22

Obsidian, 40,51,55,56
Olivine, 11,26,54,55
Onyx, 26,34
Opal, 28,54
Orthoclase, 8,46,52,55
Oxygen, 9

Pearly, 22
Peat, 15,41

Index

Pegmatite, 23,53
Peridotite, 53,55
Perlite, 40
Phosphate, 43
Phosphorite, 43
Picotite, 24
Pinacoidal, 26
Pitchstone, 56
Plagioclase, 8,46,47,52,55
Plane, 21
Plutonic, 10
Porphyry, 40,45,47,51,56
Potassium, 17
Pumice, 42,56
Pyrite, 27,54,55
Pyroxene, 29,55
Pyrrhotite, 21

Quartz, 9,17,19,25,46,47, 51,54,55
Quartzite, 17,45,47,48,51,54

Resinous, 22
Rhombohedral, 33
Rhyolite, 23,46,47,55
Rubicelle, 23

Salt, 14,35,54
Sandstone, 13,17,48,49,54
Sard, 26
Satin spar, 36
Satin spar calcite, 34
Schist, 15,20,50
Scoria, 42,47
Sedimentary, 9,11,12,54
Selenite, 35
Serpentine, 24,32,42,55
Shale, 14,15,43,44,45,54
Silica, 14,54

Silicate, 17
Silicon, 9,11
Silky, 22
Sinter, 34
Slab, 43
Slate, 24,44,45
Soapstone, 42,43
Specific gravity, 20,21
Spinel, 23,54,55
Stalactite, 28,34
Stalagmite, 34
Steatite, 42,43
Streak, 22
Striation, 27,52
Sulfur, 9,36,54
Syenite, 8,52,55

Talc, 19,50
Texture, 15
Topaz, 19,23,55
Tourmaline, 24,54
Trachite, 46
Travertine, 34,45,48
Tremolite, 20,29
Tufa, 34
Tuff, 41,43,44,47

Vein, 25,53
Violan, 29,55
Vitreous, 22
Vitrophyre, 40
Volcanic, 10,11
Volcano, 10

Waxy, 22
Wollastonite, 17
Wood, 28

Zircon, 55